CONTENTS

My Adidas Coloring Book
By Troy Davinci

Disclaimer: We are not affiliated with the Adidas in anyway, shape, or form. This Book is to be used for entertainment purposes only. All icons, graphics, Etc are original graphics and designs of Narleyapps Inc. Follow us at @Jordancoloringbook. cloloringbooklifecom and Download our app sneaker game Sneaker Match Mania. Copyright 2017 Davinci Publishing INC

YEEZY BOOST 350 "Turtle Dove"

YEEZY BOOST 350 "Turtle Dove"

YEEZY WAVE RUNNER

YEEZY WAVE RUNNER

YEEZY BOOST

NMD CITY SOCK

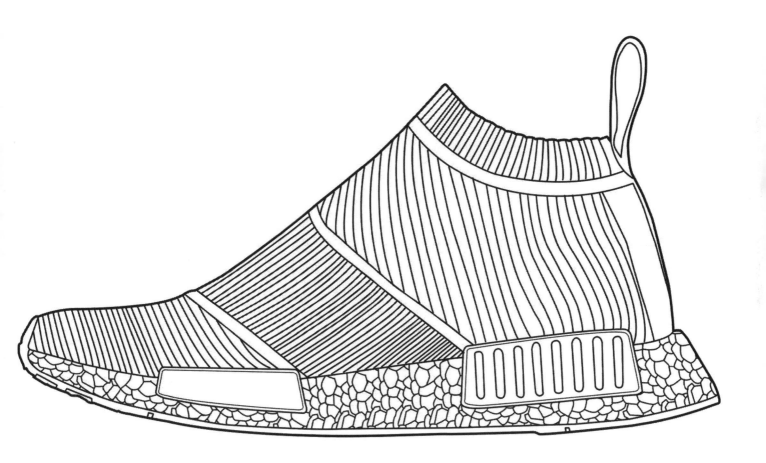

NMD CITY SOCK

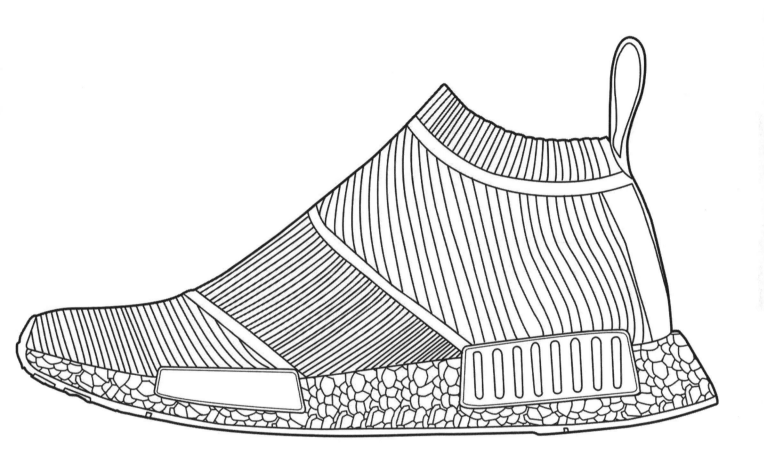

NMD

NMD

NMD R2 WHITE MOUNTAINEERING

NMD R2 WHITE MOUNTAINEERING

NMD XR1

NMD XR1

NMD CITY SOCK 2

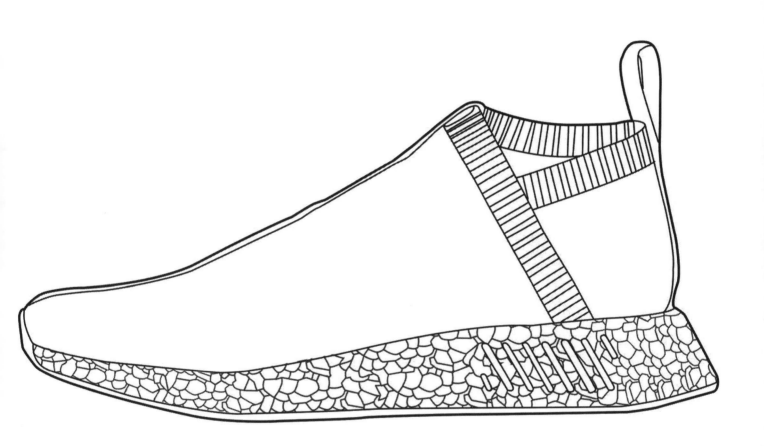

NMD CITY SOCK 2

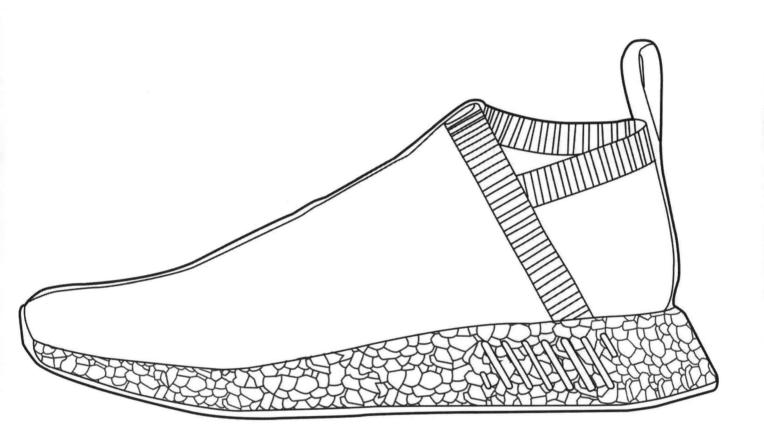

PHARRELL WILLIAMS TENNIS HU

PHARRELL WILLIAMS TENNIS HU

TUBULAR DOOM

TUBULAR DOOM

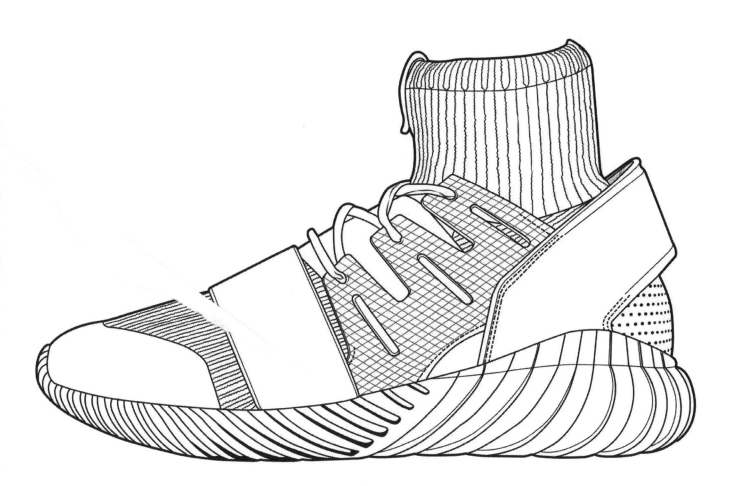

TUBULAR INVADER STRAP

TUBULAR INVADER STRAP

TUBULAR NOVA CARDBOARD

TUBULAR NOVA CARDBOARD

EQT SUPPORT ADV

EQT SUPPORT ADV

EQT SUPPORT 93/17

EQT SUPPORT 93/17

EQT SUPPORT RF PRIMEKNIT

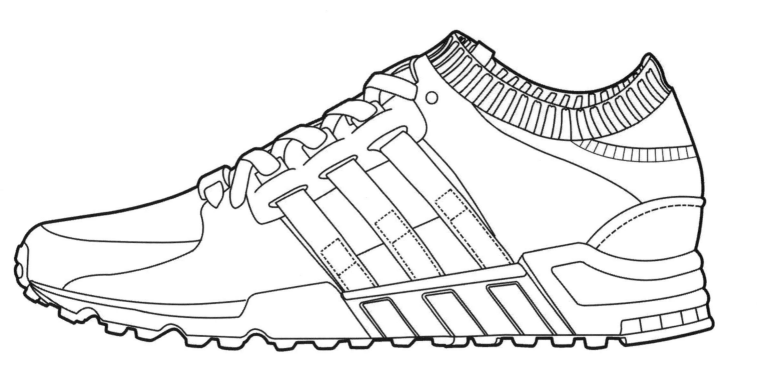

EQT SUPPORT RF PRIMEKNIT

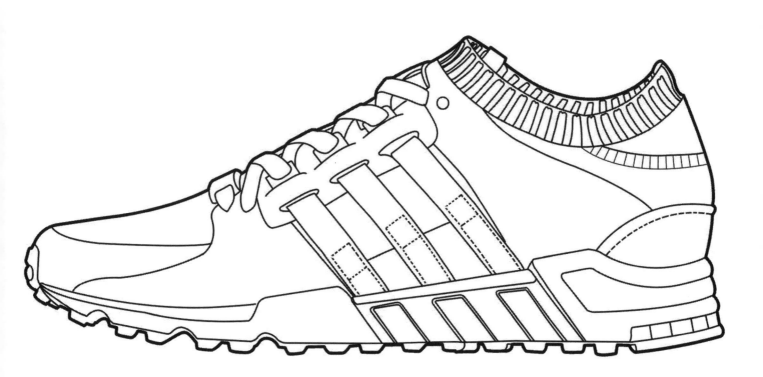

TOP TEN HI

TOP TEN HI

SUPER STAR

SUPER STAR

JEREMY SCOTT WINGS 2 0

JEREMY SCOTT WINGS 2 0

JEREMY SCOTT WINGS 3 0

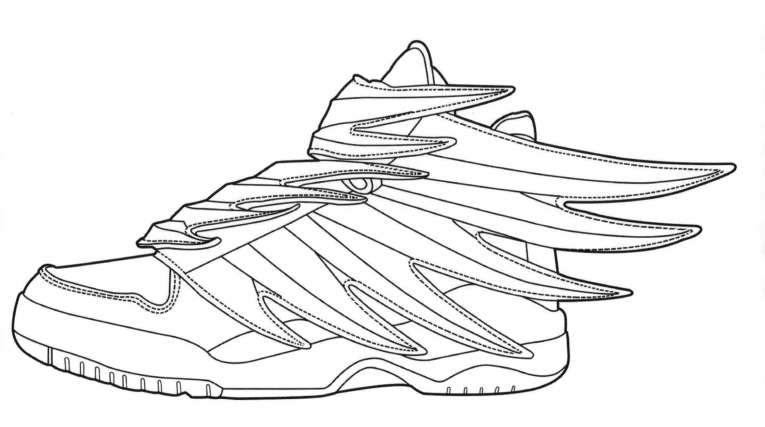

JEREMY SCOTT WINGS 3 0

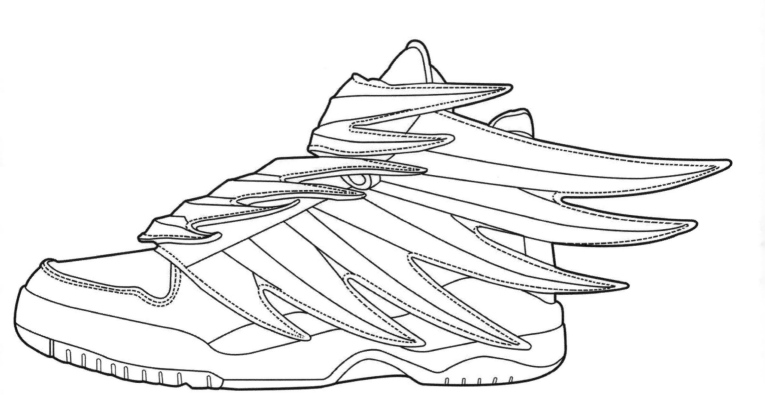

ZX-8000-BOOST

ZX-8000-BOOST

ADO ULTRA BOOST

ADO ULTRA BOOST

ULTRA BOOST UNCAGED

ULTRA BOOST UNCAGED

PURECONTROL ULTRA BOOST

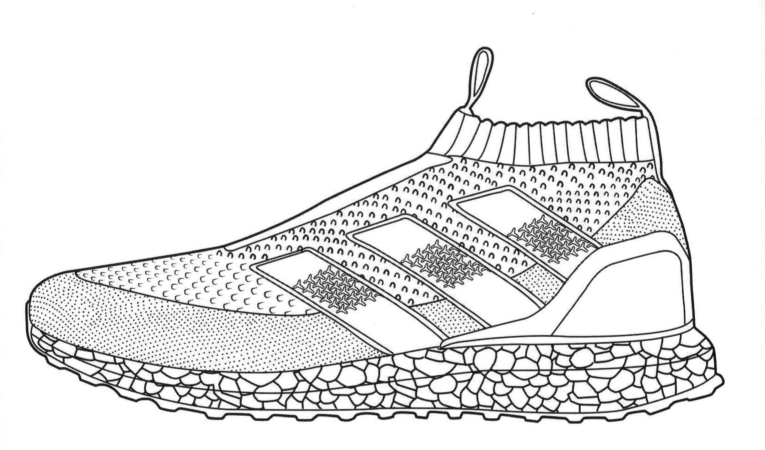

PURECONTROL ULTRA BOOST

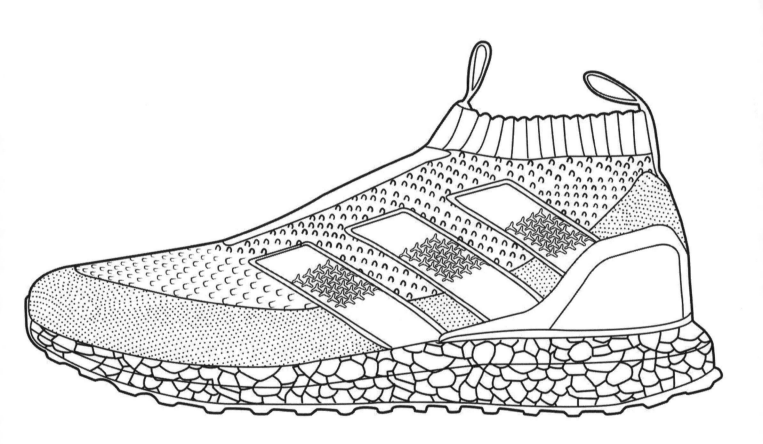

ULTRA BOOST - W.W. "WOOD WOOD

ULTRA BOOST - W.W. "WOOD WOOD

CONSORTIUM WOOD WOOD
ULTRABOOST

CONSORTIUM WOOD WOOD
ULTRABOOST

Y3 PURE BOOTS ZG

Y3 PURE BOOTS ZG

Y3 PRIMEKNIT PURE BOOST ZG

Y3 PRIMEKNIT PURE BOOST ZG

INIKI RUNNER PRIDE OF THE 70S

INIKI RUNNER PRIDE OF THE 70S

JAMES HARDEN VOL.1

JAMES HARDEN VOL.1

ZX-FLUX

ZX-FLUX

CRAZY 1 ADV

CRAZY 1 ADV

PUSHA T ULTRA BOOST EQT

PUSHA T ULTRA BOOST EQT

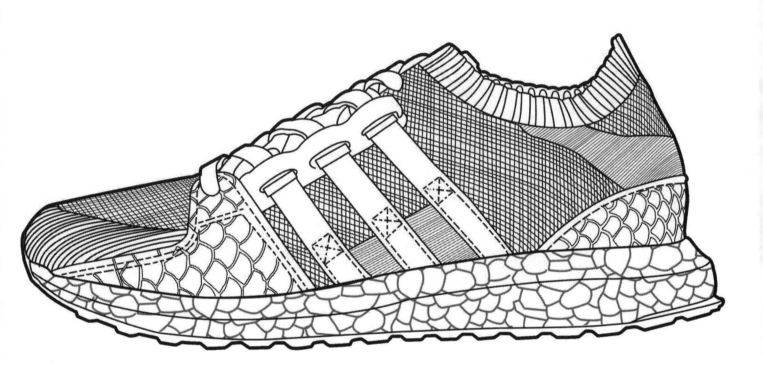

Thank you for your order
Check out our other books

ColoringBookLife.Com

Printed in Great Britain
by Amazon